THE GREAT WAR OF 1914–18 WAS PROCLAIMED BY MANY AS 'THE war to end all wars', but might better have been described as 'the war to change all wars' – this, after all, was a thoroughly modern war. It marked a definite watershed between the tactics and weaponry used in the nineteenth century and those required for twentieth-century warfare. An immaculately upright thin red line of advancing British soldiers wouldn't last long against a machine-gun position. The armies and navies engaged in the conflict could field the most technologically advanced equipment that had ever gone into battle – steel warships powered by turbine engines and armed with naval guns that could hit a target twenty miles away, poison gas, motorcycles and cars, torpedo-equipped submarines, tanks, radio communications and the greatest innovation of them all – aeroplanes.

The development, especially of fighter aircraft, from the outbreak of the war to its conclusion was astonishingly rapid. In 1914, the Royal Flying Corps, one of the forerunners of the RAF, was equipped with a few unarmed aircraft that looked like little more than the flimsy powered hang-gliders nowadays flown by weekend enthusiasts. By 1918, the RAF was the largest, best-equipped air force in the world flying fast, highly manoeuvrable, robust, well-armed modern fighters such as the SE5A, the Sopwith Camel or the Sopwith Snipe. With the end of the war, however, aircraft development programmes ground to a halt.

The Sopwith Snipe was the RAF's most advanced fighter of World War I, entering service in September 1918.

Flight Lieutenant Boothman stands in the open cockpit of the Supermarine S6B, the aircraft in which he won the Schneider Tropy seaplane race for Britain. This was the third time in a row that Supermarine aircraft had won the race for Britain.

Fifteen years later, the RAF was still equipped with open-cockpit biplane fighters that looked little different from those the pilots had flown over the Western Front. The Hawker Fury, which entered service in 1931, was at that time the finest of the RAF's fighters, capable of over 200 mph, but it was still very obviously derived from its WWI ancestors. Although the biplanes had been developed to an admirable standard, there had been no real revolution in design. But that revolution was on its way. Air Chief Marshal Sir John Salmond and Air Vice-Marshal Hugh Dowding had known each other for over twenty years. Salmond had actually taught Dowding to fly at the Central Flying School prior to the outbreak of WWI. These men were the force behind the drive for change. Both viewed recent international developments in aviation with grave concern.

The Schneider Trophy Races, an international event for seaplanes in which the RAF had been involved, had seen the Supermarine S6B monoplane claim the title outright for Britain in 1931 with an average speed around the course of more than 340 mph. The S6B went on to set an overall air speed record of 407.5 mph, although this was superseded two years later by the Italian MC-72 monoplane, a former Schneider Trophy racer, at over 440 mph. Land-based sporting monoplanes in America were regularly racing at speeds up to 300 mph and in Germany Willy Messerschmitt was working on his M37 sporting monoplane that would eventually become the Bf108, a forerunner of the famous Bf109 fighter. No biplane fighter with its fixed undercarriage, struts and supports would ever be streamlined enough to keep up with the next generation of aircraft. Clearly, something had to be done to bring the RAF fully up to date.

The result of Salmond and Dowding's desire for a modern fighter aircraft was Air Ministry specification F.5/34. This twenty-page document was at the heart of a programme to reform, expand and modernize the RAF. It called for manufacturers to submit proposals for a monoplane aircraft with a closed cockpit, retractable undercarriage, a speed in excess of 300 mph and an armament of eight machine-guns. This was four times the firepower a fighter was traditionally expected to carry but the high speeds predicted for aerial combat in the future would mean that an enemy aircraft would be in a pilot's sights for only an instant. The more guns that fired during the brief burst on target, the more hits there would be.

Salmond and Dowding were not alone in recognizing the need for a high-speed fighter. Aircraft manufacturers Supermarine and Hawker (formerly Sopwith) both had monoplane designs under way, although each company's top designers had also previously produced less than satisfactory monoplane fighter designs.

At Supermarine, Chief Designer R. J. Mitchell had come up with the Type 224, a gull-wing monoplane with an open cockpit and fixed landing gear housed in spats or streamlined fairings. Powered by a Rolls-Royce Goshawk engine, the prototype first flew in 1933, but could manage only a disappointing 228 mph.

Hawker's Chief Designer, Sydney Camm, had suggested a 'Fury Monoplane' in 1933, also with fixed landing gear shrouded by spats and also powered by the Goshawk engine. This engine was far from reliable but Rolls-Royce had an alternative under development, and Camm was advised to rethink the 'Fury Monoplane' idea pending the arrival of Rolls-Royce's new powerplant.

It must have come as something of a relief to Mitchell and Camm that neither of their original monoplane proposals progressed, for each already had in mind far more radical ideas for a new fighter.

Air Ministry specification F.5/34, inviting manufacturers to submit their proposals for a high-speed, single-seat, eight-gun fighter aircraft with enclosed cockpit and retractable undercarriage.

40 A.

Reference No. 326870/34/R.D.A.3.

AIR MINISTRY.
DIRECTORATE OF TECHNICAL DEVELOPMENT.
CONFIDENTIAL.

This document is the property of H.M. Government.

This document is intended for the use of the recipient only and may be used only in connection with work carried out for or on behalf of H.M. Government. The unauthorised retention or destruction of this document, or the disclosure of its contents to any unauthorised person, is forbidden.

Attention is hereby called to the fact that failure to comply with any one of the above instructions is an infraction of the Official Secrets Act.

Note:- Any person other than the authorised holder upon obtaining possession of this document should forward it together with his name and address in a closed envelope to THE SECRETARY, AIR MINISTRY, KINGSWAY, LONDON, W.C.2. Letter postage need not be prepaid; other postage will be refunded.

Specification No. F.5/34.

Single-seat Fighter.

Specification of Particular Requirements to accompany the Contract Agreement.

This Specification is to be regarded for contract purposes as forming part of the Contract Agreement and being subject to the same general conditions.

Approved by: (Signed) J. S. Buchanan,

for Director of Technical Development.

Deputy Director,

Date: 16th November, 1934.

Sydney Camm's approach was to take the tried and tested techniques used in biplane construction and apply them to a modern monoplane design. His new aircraft, to be called the Hurricane, had a low-slung, immensely strong wing that could easily accommodate the required eight machine-guns, and two widely spaced forward landing wheels that retracted by folding inwards towards the belly of the aircraft. The wings were covered with fabric, just like those of a biplane, as was the rear fuselage. Constructed using the same truss-girder principles as those employed in biplane manufacture, the rear fuselage was formed by four steel 'longerons' interconnected with steel and duralumin tubes. This formed the backbone of the aircraft with the whole structure then internally braced by taut steel wires. Transverse wooden formers were then attached to mke the shape, followed by longitudinal 'stringers', after which the fuselage from just aft of the cockpit back to the tail was covered with stretched fabric.

This might not seem like cutting-edge technology but the aircraft was immensely strong, and Camm knew that by using this technique, which required no welding, the Hurricane would be quick and cheap to manufacture as well as quick and easy for ground crews to repair when battle-damaged aircraft limped back to base. The wings, designed to be easily detachable so the aircraft could be handled more easily for workshop maintenance on the ground, were also fabric covered, although these would later be metal-skinned to improve performance.

The engine was supported by a metal framework and the whole of this forward section of the fuselage was clad in metal panels, again swiftly detachable to enable easy access for maintenance.

The Hurricane's fuselage was divided into bays with fireproof bulkheads separating the cockpit from the engine bay, the main fuel tanks in the wing roots, and the reserve tank situated just behind the engine. The bulkhead was sealed to stop fumes from the engine leaking into the cockpit, a potentially disastrous hazard, especially when the sliding glass cockpit canopy was closed. The pilot's seat was fixed to the fuselage structure, with no proper floor in the cockpit, and the area behind the pilot's head was strengthened to try to provide some protection should the aircraft flip over on the ground.

The newly developed Browning .303-inch calibre machine-guns (built in Britain under licence from the US factory) were not ready to be fitted for the first flight of the prototype, which was delivered from the factory in Kingston upon Thames, Surrey, to Hawker's hangar at Brooklands late in October 1935. The aircraft, serial number K5083, had gleaming metal panels and a dull silver body, the fabric having been treated with silver dope to make it stronger and airtight. It had not yet been painted in any of the now familiar Hurricane camouflage schemes. The prototype was still very much recognizable as a Hurricane, despite its rather awkward-looking two-bladed propeller, and on 5 November 1935 Hawker's Chief Test Pilot, Flight Lieutenant Bullman, taxied out onto the runway at Brooklands to take K5083 up for its first test flight.

The Hawker Hurricane prototype K5083 on the runway at Brooklands prior to its maiden flight in November 1935.

Supermarine had been building aircraft at their base on the River Itchen near Southampton for twenty years by the time R. J. Mitchell started working on their new fighter design. Supermarine's aircraft had, in the main, been flying boats and, even though some of these had been supplied to the RAF, the company was not really equipped for the mass production of aeroplanes, most of its output being hand-built by the workforce. The skill of the craftsmen at Supermarine was evident in the quality of the S6B Schneider Trophy winner that Mitchell had designed, and he knew that they could produce a highly advanced fighter design to an exacting standard. This confidence led him to specify a monocoque (literally 'single skin') design where the aluminium panels that covered the aircraft would provide much of the aircraft's structural strength. The Spitfire would still have a skeleton of metal longerons, ribs and stringers to provide its shape, but the skin, unlike the fabric covering of the Hurricane, would withstand huge amounts of stress, making it more manoeuvrable at higher speeds. Another advantage was that it allowed the wing to be thinner, reducing drag. The Spitfire's wing was immensely strong, with a metal box section beneath the skin along the leading edge and a main spar of hollow sections that fitted one inside the other, tapering off towards the tip. Its distinctive elliptical shape would further enhance the aircraft's performance.

Reginald Joseph Mitchell trained as an engineer before joining the Supermarine company in 1916, where he became chief engineer and designed their Schneider Trophy-winning seaplanes.

The inside of the Spitfire's fuselage, unlike that of the Hurricane, was unobstructed, with no need for the Hurricane's essential cross-members and steel-cable bracing. This helped to make the Spitfire far lighter than the Hurricane. The two aircraft differed in a number of other ways, too. The Hurricane's landing gear retracted inwards towards the wing roots while the Spitfire's folded outwards into the wings, with the retractor gear nearer the fuselage, helping to keep the wing as slim as possible. The wider track of the Hurricane's undercarriage, on the other hand, made it a much more forgiving aircraft to land. Neither did the Spitfire carry fuel in its wings, the fuel tanks being located between the engine and the cockpit. The first Hurricane had a retracting tail wheel while the Spitfire prototype had no tail wheel at all, just a skid. Both aircraft, however, were powered by the Rolls-Royce's new PV12 engine, later called the Merlin, and both were armed with eight Browning .303-calibre machine-guns.

The Spitfire was, at this stage, still only known by a code number, although Supermarine toyed with the idea of calling it the Shrew. Spitfire was the name that had been given to the Type 224, but it was eventually adopted for the new design, too. The complexity of its design meant that the Spitfire took longer to build than the Hurricane and the prototype was not ready until the early spring of 1936. Spitfire prototype K5054 was to take to the air for the first time with Supermarine's Chief Test Pilot 'Mutt' Summers at the controls on 5 March 1936, at Eastleigh airport near Southampton.

R. J. Mitchell's Spitfire prototype K5054 undergoing flight tests in March 1936. Note the tail skid that had yet to be replaced with a wheel.

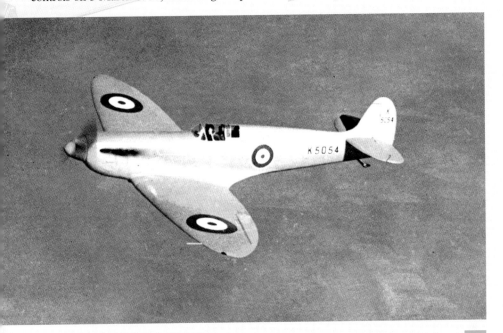

The Hurricane evaluation report written by Squadron Leader 'Downwind Johnny' Gillan, shortly after 111 Squadron received their first aircraft.

The new Browning guns were not ready for the Hurricane's maiden flight at Brooklands, so K5083 was equipped with ballast to the same weight as the guns. Despite some problems with the 1,025-horsepower Merlin engine, Flight Lieutenant Bullman guided the Hurricane into the sky and performed some basic manoeuvres, taking the aircraft to 315mph - a remarkable speed for a fighter in 1936. Bullman found the handling of the new aeroplane so good that when he landed he is reported to have said to Sydney Camm, 'Another winner here, I think!' Rolls-Royce immediately set to work correcting the faults with the engine, developing it into the Merlin II, and over the next few months a variety of improvements were made to K5083. The engine exhausts were altered to face rearwards, the lower fairings attached to the landing gear were abandoned as they were prone to damage when taxiing on grass, and the tail wheel became fixed rather than retractable. A small fin was added below the tail, around the wheel, to aid in spin recovery, bracing struts for the tailplane were deleted, and the outer sections of the wings were slightly swept to help improve the Hurricane's centre of gravity. The Hurricane's first flight came shortly after the maiden flight at Augsburg in Germany of Messerschmitt's Bf109 prototype, ironically temporarily powered by a specially imported Rolls-Royce Kestrel engine, the fighter that would become such a dreaded adversary. The new Hawker fighter's maiden flight also came just before that of its greatest ally, the Spitfire.

The 1936 Air Ministry flight-test report on the Spitfire from the Aeroplane and Armament Experimental Establishment at Martlesham Heath.

By the time 'Mutt' Summers raced down the runway at Eastleigh in K5054, Rolls-Royce had ironed out some of the teething problems with their new engine, and the prototype Spitfire was powered by a Merlin II. For the first flight, Summers made a few circuits of the airfield, leaving the landing gear down while checking the controls and general handling characteristic of the aeroplane. He was watched anxiously by R. J. Mitchell and his team, but when he landed he climbed out of the aircraft and famously stated, 'I don't want anything touched.' Clearly he was pleased with the way the first flight had gone, but his comment was probably more of a request to the technicians not to change any of the settings than a pronouncement that the Spitfire was perfect. In fact, a number of changes were made following subsequent test flights, including the fitting of a new type of propeller before K5054 was tested for top speed. R. J. Mitchell, by this time seriously ill with cancer, had estimated that the top speed of the Spitfire (a name which he claimed never to like) would be 350mph; the prototype achieved just under 349mph.

Towards the end of May 1936 K5054 was delivered to the government Aeroplane and Armament Experimental Establishment at Martlesham Heath, near Ipswich, for trials and evaluation. So impressed were they with the new fighter that, within a week, before the test reports were properly complete, Supermarine received its first production order from the RAF for 310 Spitfires.

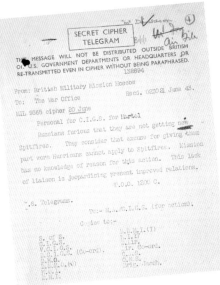

Above and right: These official memos form part of a stream of WWII correspondence between Britain and the Soviet Union following the Russians' complaints that they were being sent sub-standard Spitfires and Hurricanes.

The Hurricane went through its trials at Martelsham Heath at around the same time and in June 1936 an order was placed with Hawker for 600 aircraft. The Hurricane was seen as being more robust than the Spitfire as its construction followed the same principles as the biplanes that had been in service for so long. No problems were envisaged, therefore, in training ground crews and workshop technicians to effect speedy repairs to battle damage. Neither was it expected that there would be any reason why the Hurricane could not quickly replace the older designs on Hawker's production lines. Adapting the framework around the engine to accept the new Merlin II installation did cause a slight delay, but the first forty Hurricanes were ready for delivery to No. 111 Squadron at Northolt in Middlesex in December 1937, making the Hurricane the first of the RAF's new eight-gun monoplane fighters to enter service. In February 1938, 111 Squadron's commanding officer, Squadron Leader John Gillan, flew his Hurricane from Turnhouse, just outside Edinburgh, all the way to Northolt, on the western outskirts of London, in a mere forty-eight minutes. Though helped by a strong following wind, he achieved an average speed of an incredible 408.75mph, earning himself the nickname 'Downwind Johnny'.

By now the threat of war hung heavy over Europe and manufacture of the Hurricane became a major priority, with modifications being made to the design on the production line to give the aircraft metal-skinned wings and a new three-blade propeller. This necessitated further adaptations to the Merlin engine but gave the aeroplane an increased top speed of around 328 mph in level flight.

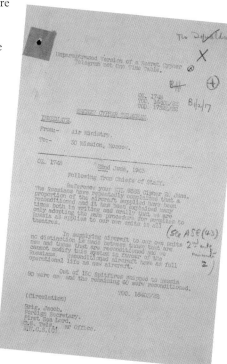

By contrast, production of the Spitfire proved to be a real headache for Supermarine. Turning a bespoke thoroughbred like K5054 into a machine suitable for mass manufacture was no easy task. The complex structure, especially the wings, proved slow to build in quantity and this, in turn, led many to wonder if the Spitfire would ever be a practical combat aircraft. Damage to a Hurricane would be easily repairable, but getting a Spitfire back in the air looked as though it might be impossible for hard-pressed ground crews. Further adding to Supermarine's troubles, R. J. Mitchell succumbed to cancer and died in June 1937. Supermarine persuaded the Air Ministry that they could streamline production, subcontractors were brought up to speed and the first production-line Spitfire was delivered to No. 19 Squadron, based at Duxford, on 4 August 1938.

A little over a year later, in September 1939, Germany plunged Europe into war and the RAF was still woefully under-equipped with its new fighters. Only around 500 Hurricanes had been delivered to 19 RAF squadrons and fewer than 200 Spitfires had been produced for 10 squadrons. Putting his experience in the mass manufacture of motor cars to good use, Lord Nuffield was appointed to organize production of the thousands of new aircraft that were now urgently required. A new Spitfire factory was established in the Midlands, the Gloster Aircraft Company began producing Hurricanes, as did the Canadian Car and Foundry Company in Thunder Bay, Ontario.

Three female fitters pose for a propaganda photograph 'working' on a new Hurricane. Note the orange fuel tank in the wing root.

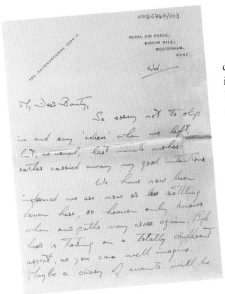

ROYAL AIR FORCE,
BIGGIN HILL,
WESTERHAM,
KENT.

Hurricanes and Spitfires were deployed against the German Luftwaffe in France in the early part of the war, but they could do little to prevent the rout of the British Expeditionary Force. Air Chief Marshal Sir Hugh Dowding, now in charge of Fighter Command, wisely resisted committing too many aircraft to the Battle of France, preserving as many fighters as possible to defend Britain against the expected German onslaught. Nevertheless, of the 261 Hurricanes sent to France, 195 were lost before the evacuation from Dunkirk, as were 67 Spitfires. The Spitfires especially, however, had given a good account of themselves against the Luftwaffe's Bf109, and these two would continue to battle for supremacy of performance as new variants were developed during the course of the war.

Just as the Allies were evacuated from France, so too were they recalled from Norway where No. 46 Squadron's Hurricanes had been deployed. The Hurricanes did not have the range to be flown home but rather than destroy them on the ground in the face of the German advance, the RAF pilots bravely landed their aircraft on the deck of the carrier HMS *Glorious*, despite having no experience of deck landings and without the aid of the arrester hooks normally fitted to naval aircraft. Sadly, their efforts were in vain as the Hurricanes were all lost when the carrier was sunk en route to Scapa Flow by the German battleship *Scharnhorst*. Valuable lessons had, however, been learnt in France and Norway that would stand the RAF in good stead for the coming Battle of Britain.

Spitfire pilot Pilot Officer Roy Mottram, based at Biggin Hill, sent this letter about his experiences in the Battle of Britain to Section Officer 'Bunty' Nash from his previous base at Pembrey.

The Messerschmitt Bf109 had a stressed-skin construction similar to the Spitfire and entered service with the Luftwaffe in 1937.

Some of 92 Squadron's pilots
(Roy Mottram second from left)
and, inset, 'Bunty' Nash.

The Germans knew that they had to eliminate the threat from the RAF before they could consider mounting any kind of invasion of Britain, so the Luftwaffe's priority when they launched their air offensive was to destroy RAF aircraft and cripple their bases. Hurricanes and Spitfires formed the backbone of Britain's air defences. Guided by the network of coastal radar stations, they scrambled to intercept the massed formations of German bombers and fighters. The tactics were generally for the Hurricanes to concentrate on attacking the bombers while the more agile Spitfires, when they were available (Hurricanes still outnumbered Spitfires at least two to one), took on the German escort fighters. The Battle of Britain raged from mid-July 1940 to mid-September with a devastating rate of attrition. During the second two weeks in August the RAF and the Luftwaffe lost a combined total of 800 aircraft, with the balance slightly in the RAF's favour. The culmination of the battle came on 15 September when London was targeted by two major Luftwaffe attacks each involving around 250 aircraft. The RAF's Hurricanes and Spitfires accounted for at least 124 German bombers and 53 fighters for the loss of 25 RAF aircraft. The Germans realized that they could not win the Battle of Britain and concentrated thereafter on night-time air raids.

Fighter Command's only VC of the Battle of Britain was won by Flight Lieutenant James Nicolson.

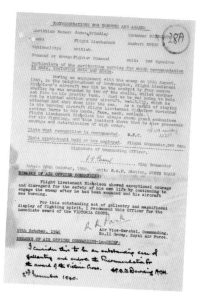

Essential to the defeat of the Luftwaffe in the Battle of Britain were the supplies of new aircraft being delivered in quantity to the RAF – the Luftwaffe could not replace its losses as quickly and began to lose its numerical superiority. For both sides, of course, the loss of trained pilots was far more of a problem, but an RAF pilot who crash-landed or parachuted to safety could expect to be back in the air in a new machine almost straight away. And the new Hurricanes and Spitfires were constantly being improved. Armour plating was fitted to protect the pilots and engines, 20-mm cannon supplemented the machine guns, control surfaces were covered with aluminium rather than fabric to improve manoeuvrability and the Merlin engine received endless tweaks to increase its power and reliability.

Because of its advanced construction, the Spitfire was the easier aircraft to upgrade in terms of performance. The first aircraft in 1938 equipped with a 990-horsepower Merlin engine achieved nearly 350 mph while the final versions in 1948 had 2,340 horsepower Rolls-Royce Griffon powerplants and could top 450 mph. The ultimate Spitfire, known as the Spiteful, was capable of almost 500 mph.

The Spitfire was more complicated for ground staff to deal with and accidents were common at first as pilots unused to retractable landing gear forgot to lower it. A warning klaxon was fitted to remind them.

Although it began to lag further behind the Spitfire in terms of performance as WWII progressed, the Hurricane proved far more adaptable. Its thicker wing meant that it could accommodate cannon more successfully than the Spitfire; it became the 'Hurribomber' when a 250-pound bomb was carried under each wing; it carried drop tanks to extend its range; and could be fitted with anti-tank guns and racks of rockets to turn it into a ground-attack aircraft while still maintaining a useful function as a fighter. At sea the Hurricane was launched from the decks of merchant ships by rocket-propelled catapult to protect convoys (the pilot then had to ditch in the sea as recovery to a ship was impossible); served with special sand filters on its air intakes in the heat of the North African deserts and with special skids on its undercarriage in the Russian Arctic.

Although it was withdrawn from front-line service as a fighter in Europe from 1942 onwards, the Hurricane was still fulfilling that role in Burma and the Far East right up to 1945. Yet while it continued to serve with other air forces around the world for several years, the very last of the RAF's Hurricanes were withdrawn from service in Palestine in 1947. The invaluable role played by the aircraft was proven by analysis after WWII which showed that Hurricanes had shot down more enemy aircraft during the Battle of Britain than all other aircraft types and the anti-aircraft batteries put together. The Hurricane also served in more theatres of war than any other type of aircraft.

Just like the retractable landing gear, closed cockpits took some time to get used to, many pilots preferring to fly with them open.

The Hurricane's versatility may have made it seem more of a workhorse to the Spitfire's thoroughbred, but the Spitfire was nothing if not adaptable. Like the Hurricane, the Spitfire, with suitable modifications, served in the dry heat of the desert and the intense humidity of the tropics. Both marques were also developed as carrier-borne fighters (naval versions were known as the Sea Hurricane and Seafire) and experiments were even conducted in fitting Spitfires and Hurricanes with floats so that they could be used as seaplanes, taking the Spitfire right back to its Schneider Trophy roots. The last of the RAF's front-line Spitfires were retired in 1951, although some were used for reconnaissance work up to 1954 and three were kept for meteorological work until 1957. By then the speed of the new jets far outpaced the Spitfire, despite the fact that one was once recorded diving at Mach 0.92 (around 600 mph). Spitfires were sold to a number of foreign countries including Egypt and Israel, who, in 1948, pitted Spitfires against other Spitfires in combat, the Israelis also fielding ageing Messerschmitt Bf109s!

The Hurricane and the Spitfire are two of the most famous aeroplanes ever to have flown, with over 14,500 Hurricanes having been built by the time production ceased along with more than 20,000 Spitfires and Seafires. Only a handful remain in flying condition today, but they continue to thrill crowds of admirers whenever they appear at air displays, their distinguished history making them a far greater draw than even the most glamorous of the latest breed of supersonic jet fighters.

A restored Mark XIV Spitfire (left), delivered to the Royal Belgian Air Force in 1948 and now in private hands, in formation with a Mark XVI, each painted in the post-war red-and-silver colour scheme of 41 Squadron. Both are powered by Rolls-Royce Griffon engines.

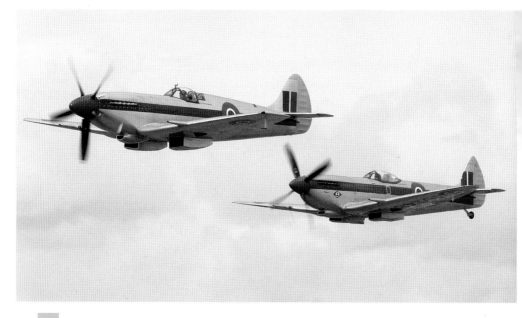